Music by MARC SHAIMAN

Lyrics by SCOTT WITTMAN & MARC SHAIMAN

HAIRSPRAY

SOUNDTRACK TO THE MOTION PICTURE

Special thanks to
Paul Broucek, Jason Cienkus, Joe Kara, PJ Loughran, Sohrab Nafici, Richard Read,
Mark Sendroff, Lori Silfen, Steve Smith, Sandeep Sriram, John F.X. Walsh

www.hairspraymovie.com
www.newlinerecords.com
For exclusive Hairspray merchandise, visit www.newlineshop.com

Alfred Publishing Co., Inc.
16320 Roscoe Blvd., Suite 100
P.O. Box 10003
Van Nuys, CA 91410-0003
alfred.com

YOU CAN'T STOP THE BEAT!

CONTENTS

GOOD MORNING BALTIMORE

Lyrics by
MARC SHAIMAN and
SCOTT WITTMAN

Music by
MARC SHAIMAN

8

Good Morning Baltimore - 8 - 5
28431

12

THE NICEST KIDS IN TOWN

Lyrics by
MARC SHAIMAN and
SCOTT WITTMAN

Music by
MARC SHAIMAN

Fast, hot and driving (♩ = 168)

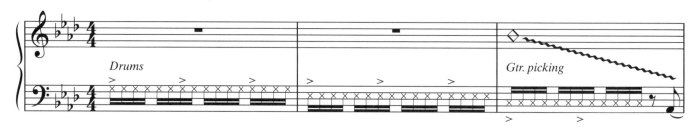

Corny: *Hey there, teenage Baltimore!*

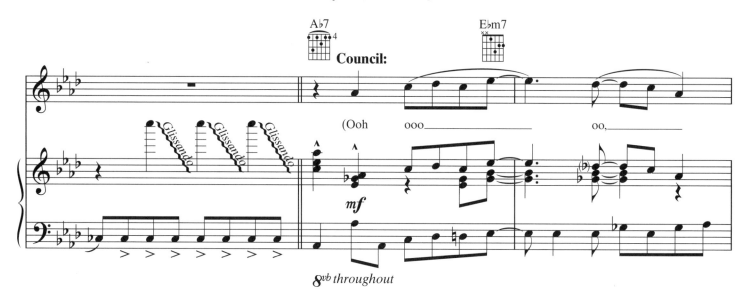

Don't change that channel! 'Cause it's time for the Corny Collins Show!

The Nicest Kids in Town - 10 - 1
28431

Brought to you by Ultra Clutch Hairspray!

squares be - hind,__ and then they shake it, shake it, shake it like they're los - ing their mind.__ You'll nev - er

see them frown__ 'cause they're the nic - est kids in town.__ (Ooh ooo__

Council:

__ oo,__ ooh ooh ooo__ ooo ooh.) Ooh,

Corny:

ev - 'ry af - ter - noon you turn your T V on.__ (Na na, na, na, na,

Council:

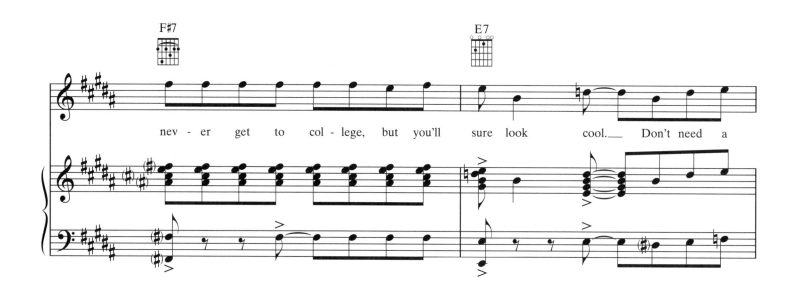

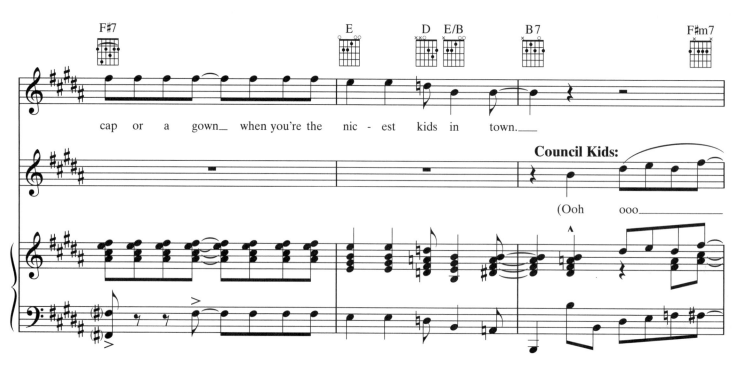

The Nicest Kids in Town - 10 - 10
28431

24

IT TAKES TWO

Lyrics by
MARC SHAIMAN and
SCOTT WITTMAN

Music by
MARC SHAIMAN

'60s rhythm ballad (♩. = 69)

1. They say it's a man's world. Well, that can-not be de-nied.
2. A king ain't a king with-out the pow'r be-hind the throne.
3. Just like Frank-ie Av-a-lon had his fa-v'rite Mouse-ke-teer,

But what good's a man's world with-out a wom-an by his side?
A prince is a pau-per, babe, with-out a chick to call his own.
I dream of a lov-er, babe, to say the things I long to hear.

It Takes Two - 4 - 1
28431

26

(The Legend of)
MISS BALTIMORE CRABS

Lyrics by
MARC SHAIMAN and
SCOTT WITTMAN

Music by
MARC SHAIMAN

34

36

I CAN HEAR THE BELLS

Lyrics by
MARC SHAIMAN and
SCOTT WITTMAN

Music by
MARC SHAIMAN

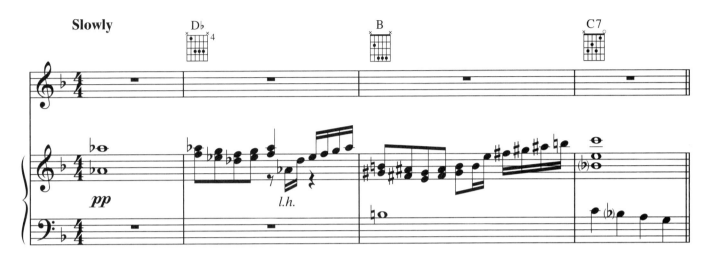

I can__ hear the bells. Well, don't 'cha__ hear 'em chime?

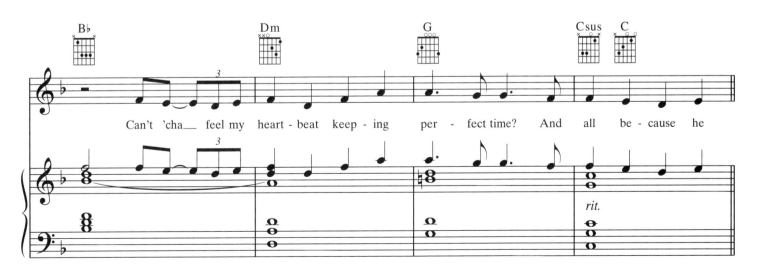

Can't 'cha__ feel my heart-beat keep-ing per - fect time? And all be-cause he

I Can Hear the Bells - 9 - 1
28431

round two, I'll primp, but___ won't be late be - cause round three's when we

kiss in - side his car. Won't go all the way, but I'll go pret - ty fa - ar.

Round four, he'll ask me___ for my hand, and then round five, we'll

book the___ wed - ding band, so by round six, Am - ber, much to your sur - prise, this

LADIES' CHOICE

Lyrics by
SCOTT WITTMAN and
MARC SHAIMAN

Music by
MARC SHAIMAN

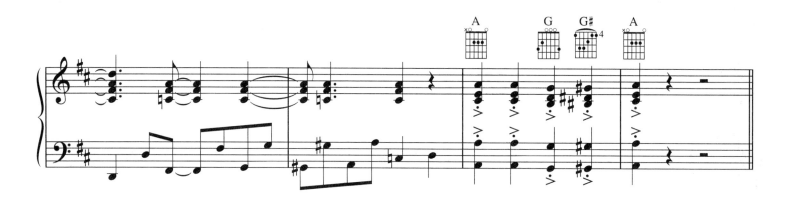

Once you've browsed through the whole se - lec - tion, shake those hips in my di - rec - tion. A

Ah ah ah.

Chorus 1:

pret - ti - er pack - age you nev - er did see. Take me home_ and then un - wrap me.

Ooh._

Ooh._

Shop a - round_ but, lit - tle dar - lin', I've got_ to be_ the la - dies'

52

55

Ladies' Choice - 10 - 8
28431

56

THE NEW GIRL IN TOWN

Lyrics by
SCOTT WITTMAN and
MARC SHAIMAN

Music by
MARC SHAIMAN

Moderately fast rock & roll (♩ = 126)

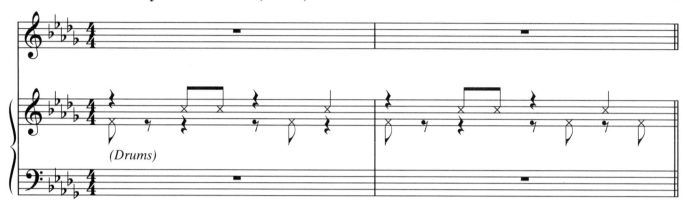

(Drums)

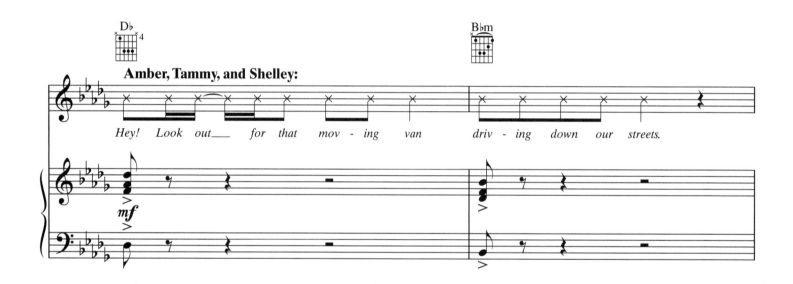

Amber, Tammy, and Shelley:

Hey! Look out___ for that mov - ing van driv - ing down our streets.

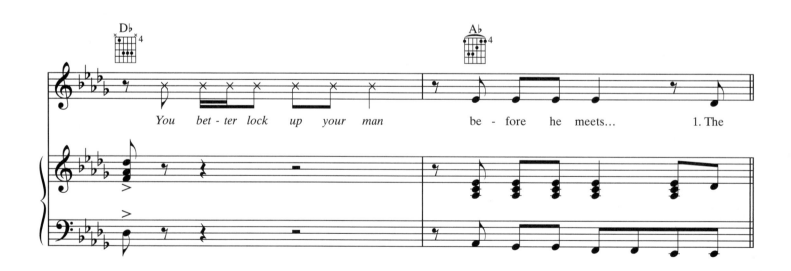

You bet - ter lock up your man be - fore he meets... 1. The

62

The New Girl in Town - 6 - 5
28431

WELCOME TO THE 60'S

Lyrics by
MARC SHAIMAN and
SCOTT WITTMAN

Music by
MARC SHAIMAN

76

RUN AND TELL THAT

Lyrics by
MARC SHAIMAN
and SCOTT WITTMAN

Music by
MARC SHAIMAN

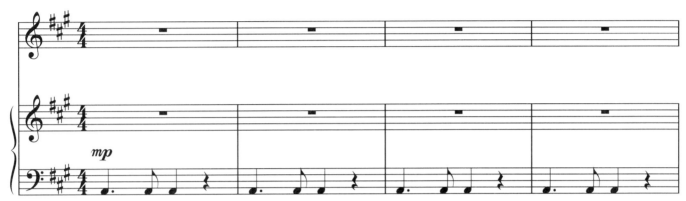

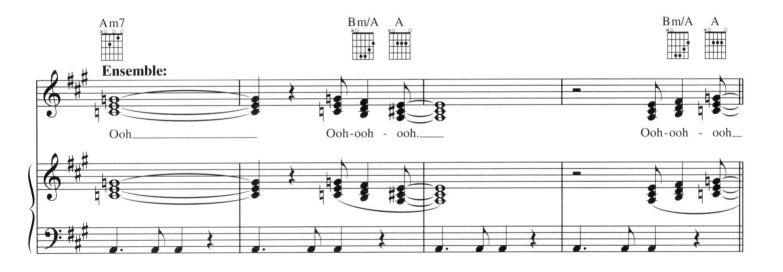

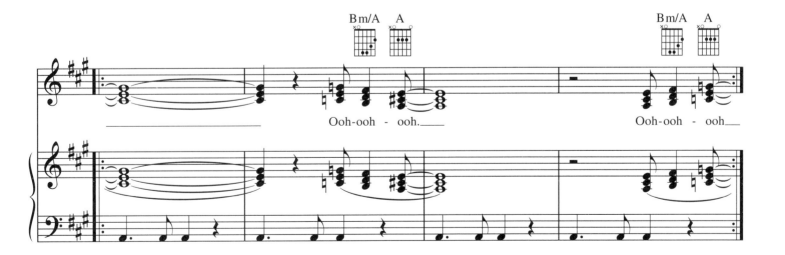

Bm/A   A

Ooh-ooh - woo!__

Seaweed:

D/A   A7   D/A   A7   D/A

I can't see__ why peo-ple   look at me__ and on-ly   see the col-or of my face.__

A   A7   D/A   A7   D/A

__   And   then there's those__ that try to   help, God knows,__ but al-ways

A7   D/A   A7   B

have to put me in my place.__   But   I won't   ask__ you to be

82

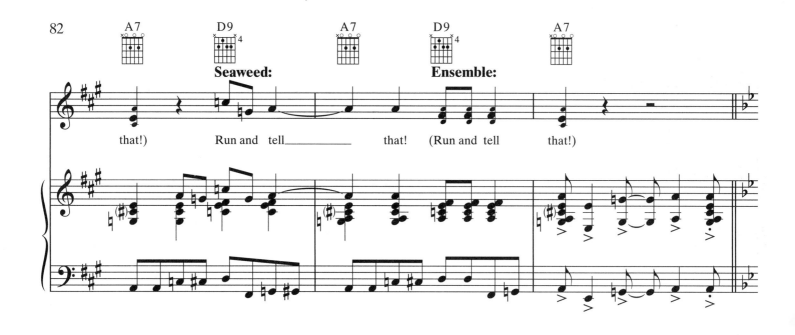

Seaweed:
Ensemble:

that!) Run and tell_____ that! (Run and tell that!)

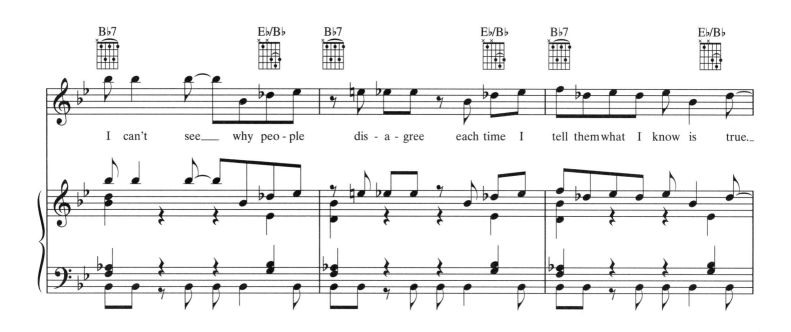

I can't see___ why peo-ple dis-a-gree each time I tell them what I know is true.___

___ And if you come and see the world I'm from, I bet your

86

Run and Tell That - 11 - 8
28431

Nature Boy

Words and Music by Eden Ahbez

BIG, BLONDE AND BEAUTIFUL

Lyrics by
MARC SHAIMAN and
SCOTT WITTMAN

Music by
MARC SHAIMAN

94

stir - ring 'til it hits___ the spot.___ Be - cause I'm

big, blonde, and beau - ti - ful.___ There___ is noth-ing 'bout us that's un -

suit - a - ble.___ Why___ sit in the bleachers tim - id and a - fraid,_ when, Ed - na,

you look like the whole___ pa - rade!___ They say that

Big, Blonde and Beautiful - 6 - 6
28431

BIG, BLONDE AND BEAUTIFUL

(Reprise)

Lyrics by
SCOTT WITTMAN and
MARC SHAIMAN

Music by
MARC SHAIMAN

Big, Blonde and Beautiful (Reprise) - 3 - 1
28341

(You're) TIMELESS TO ME

Lyrics by
MARC SHAIMAN and
SCOTT WITTMAN

Music by
MARC SHAIMAN

I KNOW WHERE I'VE BEEN

Lyrics by
MARC SHAIMAN and
SCOTT WITTMAN

Music by
MARC SHAIMAN

WITHOUT LOVE

Lyrics by
MARC SHAIMAN and
SCOTT WITTMAN

Music by
MARC SHAIMAN

1. Once I was__ a self - ish fool__ who nev - er un - der - stood.__

120

Without Love - 11 - 5
28431

124

Without Love - 11 - 9
28431

126

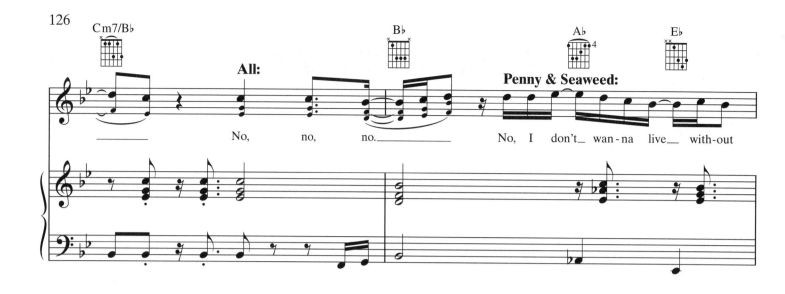

No, no, no._____ No, I don't__ wan-na live__ with-out

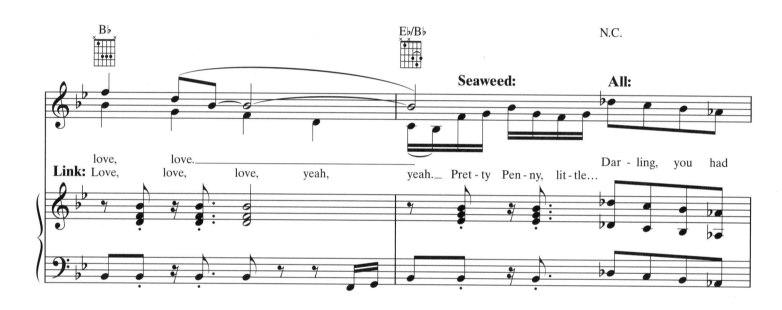

love, love._____

Link: Love, love, love, yeah, yeah.__ Pret-ty Pen-ny, lit-tle... Dar-ling, you had

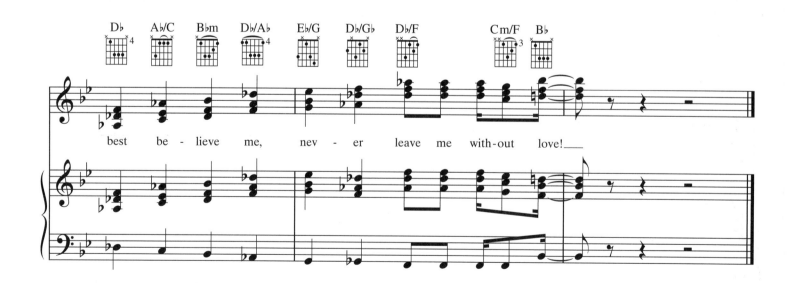

best be-lieve me, nev-er leave me with-out love!____

(IT'S) HAIRSPRAY

Lyrics by
MARC SHAIMAN and
SCOTT WITTMAN

Music by
MARC SHAIMAN

130

132

You Can't Stop the Beat

Lyrics by
MARC SHAIMAN and
SCOTT WITTMAN

Music by
MARC SHAIMAN

Brisk and exultant (♩ = 168)

You Can't Stop the Beat - 16 - 1
28431

* All male vocals written at pitch.

140

144

COME SO FAR
(Got So Far To Go)

Lyrics by
SCOTT WITTMAN and
MARC SHAIMAN

Music by
MARC SHAIMAN

1. Hey, old friend, let's look____ back on the cra-side____
2. Hey, old friend, to-geth-er side____ by side____

150

zy clothes_ we wore._____ Ain't it fun to look_
____ and year___ by year._____ The road was filled with twists_

____ back,_____ and to see____ it's all___ been done___ be - fore._
____ and turns,_ oh, but that's___ the road___ that got___ us here._

All those nights to - geth - er_____ are a spe - cial mem - o - ry,___
Let's move past the bad___ times,_____ but be - fore___ those mem - 'ries fade,_

_____ and I can't___ wait for to - mor - row,_____ just as long___
let's for - give, but not___ for - get_____ and learn_

152

156

COOTIES

Lyrics by
MARC SHAIMAN and
SCOTT WITTMAN

Music by
MARC SHAIMAN

162

163

Cooties - 6 - 6
28431

MAMA, I'M A BIG GIRL NOW

Lyrics by
MARC SHAIMAN and
SCOTT WITTMAN

Music by
MARC SHAIMAN

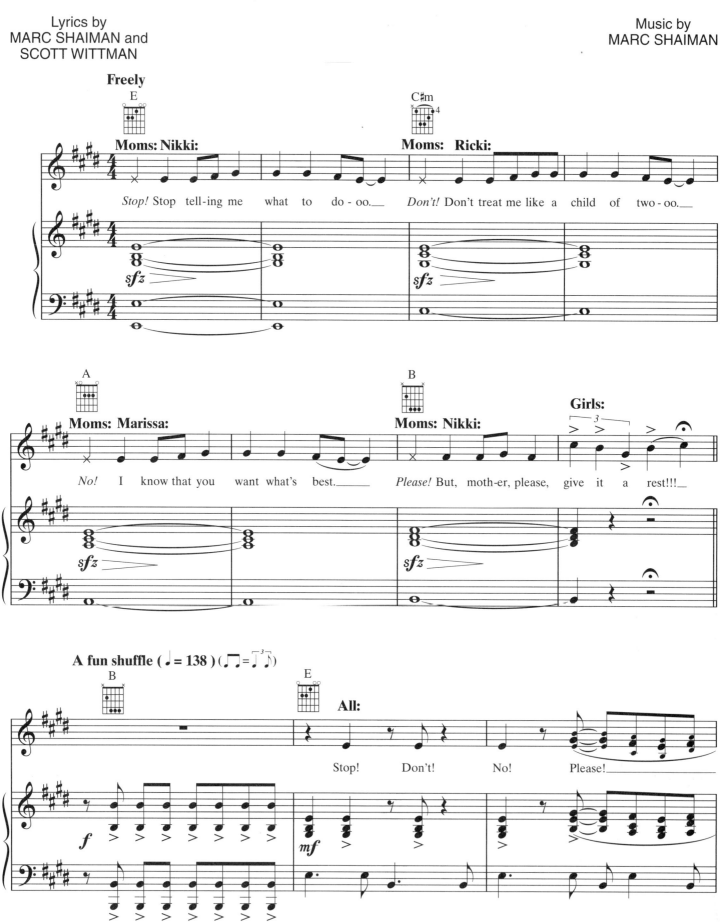

Mama, I'm a Big Girl Now - 9 - 1
28431

Stop! Don't! No! Please!_____ Stop! Don't!

No! Please!_____ Ma-ma, I'm a big girl now!

Nikki:
Once up-on a time when I was just a kid,_____ you nev-er let me do just what the

old-er kids did.___ But lose that laun-dry list of what you won't al-low,_____ 'cause

Girls:

166

Mama, I'm a Big Girl Now - 9 - 3
28431

169

172

Mama, I'm a Big Girl Now - 9 - 9
28431